IT'S NOT BLOODY ROCKET SCIENCE . . .

THE
JOURNAL

WHAT PEOPLE SAID ABOUT
IT'S NOT BLOODY ROCKET SCIENCE – THE JOURNAL

We have engaged with Dulcie to train some of the high potential leaders in our business to bring her book and her personal branch of leadership science to life. I love how this journal will help us embed our leadership development – without taking up hours of precious time. Result.

Claire Clarke, HR Director, Casual Dining Group

We invited Dulcie to present at our annual conference this year to bring her book to life. Her latest journal reflects the person we saw on stage. Down to earth, loads of bright ideas... full of relevant and well researched advice.

Mark Derry, Executive Chairman, Brasserie Bar Co Limited

I originally chose Dulcie to help us with our plans for leadership because she was the only 'expert' who told me I was wrong... and she was right! She has that rare quality of being able to convey complex theories in such a way that it resonated with everyone from our Team Leaders to our CEO. The journal will help us to embed our leadership development.

Gary Mitchell, Group HR Director EDAM Group

Innovative, empathetic and chock-full of cognitive expertise, this journal is a kindly tool for contemporary times. I had quite a few goes at CBT type stuff throughout Uni and wish that some of the professionals had nailed the same tone and warmth of the journal!

Abi Silverthorne, Freelancer – The Hollywood News

I loved Dulcie's book so much I bought a copy for everyone in my 100 strong department. This journal will mean even more people will benefit from her really grounded, down to earth way of bringing leadership science to life. It's already helping me and my team to stick to resolutions that might not have lasted past New Year's Day!

Anna-Marie Mason, Director of Brand Marketing, Mitchells & Butlers

I'm usually a grade 'A' sceptic when it comes to this type of publication. However, with a few hours to spend at an airport and the subsequent flight to Moscow, I thought I'd give it a look. First a quick flick through had me intrigued. It turned a usually tiresome journey into one of the best ever, as I read the whole journal in detail, filling in some pages as I went, mentally noting others for completion later. I was hooked. Dulcie's style and informal teachings really hit the mark with me. Being an engineer, the mix of science and "doing" is brilliant. Highly recommended for sceptics everywhere.

Chris Longstaff, VP Product Management, Mindtech Global Ltd

WHAT PEOPLE SAID ABOUT
IT'S NOT BLOODY ROCKET SCIENCE...

Dulcie has the uncanny knack of making what should be boring theory actually mean something

James Pavey, Operations Director, Tesco Hospitality

This book does contain real science and not celebrity pseudoscience about vitamins and hair...

Sarra Laycock, Chief Operations Officer, Sequani (Pharmaceuticals) Ltd

Dulcie makes us think about getting things done...a great mix of the practical and well researched.

Dennis Deare, Brand Operations Director, Mitchells and Butlers

It's a Leadership book, but not as we know it!

Dr Chris Edger, Professor of Multi-Unit Leadership,
Birmingham City University Business School

Dulcie is one of the most perceptive people I have ever worked with. She is a bloody superstar!

Matt Snell, Gusto Restaurants

Dulcie is one of those people who cuts through crap faster than the speed of light.

Kadisha Lewis Roberts, HR Director Talent and Operations AFEMEA Amcor

You probably shouldn't read this if you secretly want to stay doing what you have always done...

Mark Millet, Managing Director, Chef and Brewer Restaurants

This book will provide you with insight and understanding that you will actually remember and use.

Martyn Allen Distribution Manager, UK and Ireland Parker Ltd

She helps us unlock our potential to be infinitely better...and beyond...!

James Silverthorne, Production Director, Taylor Wimpey PLC

WHAT'S THIS JOURNAL ACTUALLY FOR?

Taking time to think about our thinking is positively good for us. There are countless studies that show that taking time out from "doing stuff" for a while and using that space to reflect, think creatively or differently, has positive implications for our mental health and our productivity.

If you don't believe that yet, try this:

A study done at Harvard split a group of workers from the same company into 2 groups. Group 1 worked as normal – 9 to 5. Group 2 stopped work at 4.45 and spent the last 15 minutes reflecting on their day – either in groups or alone. In just 9 weeks the study found that the "stop and reflect" group were generating 24% more sales than the "work flat out until the bitter end" group. Just 15 minutes less work and more thinking time per day gave them a huge, measurable benefit.[1]

Or this:

The Great Good Science Center at the exceptionally well respected University of California – Berkeley, has collected together numerous scientific studies that help us to understand the many positive health benefits of stopping the reflect about the things you are grateful for.[2] Many studies have found that regularly writing down grateful thoughts or sending a letter to someone to express gratitude can activate the feel good chemicals serotonin and dopamine. Serotonin linked drugs are most often used to treat depression. Many dopamine enhancing drugs are legal – alcohol and prescription painkillers but some aren't – Heroin and Ecstasy. The simple act of counting your blessings and writing them down, gives you access to a natural high – with none of the side effects of the clinical drugs.

That's the reason I've written this companion journal. It's Not Bloody Rocket Science explained as simply as possible some of the science and research about what makes our brains tick and how we can use that to our advantage. This journal tries to simplify things even further. There is a lot less space given up to explaining the science behind why particular activities work. Instead, there is some quick guidance and then the space to actually DO the activity. References are given to the page in It's Not Bloody Rocket Science where the particular bit of science or research that sits behind an exercise is explained. So if you want to read more, you can. But you don't need to! The activities should work just as they are and should help you to be happier and more productive.

I hope you see some good results from doing these exercises, be curious about why and want to share the science with other people. But if you don't have time for that, can't be bothered or aren't interested in why this stuff works then the journal can stand alone. You can use these pages to just get on with it!

1. INBRS **P.153**
2. THE SCIENCE OF GRATITUDE – UC BERKELEY

HERE ARE THE RULES:
THERE AREN'T ANY!

This book is not designed to begin at the beginning and finish at the end. You can use it like that if you want to and that approach will work great, but if that doesn't float your boat, feel free to browse and choose whichever page takes your fancy at any given time.

Following the Contents page is a section Specific Activities For Particular Situations. This shows which activities might be most useful to help you reflect when you have a particular issue. So, if you are feeling overwhelmed about how much you have to do it suggests, for example, The 4 Ds or Just Take 10 activities might help. Or, if you are about to begin a new job or project, First 100 Days or Success Beyond My Wildest Dreams could kick start your thinking.

This is your thinking time. By all means, skip to the end and work backwards. Flick it open at random each day. It's your brain and your rules!

Some studies say we reflect better when we are fresh. Some say we are at our best when we are thinking about the day just past. I say do it whenever you want. I have just 2 pieces of advice:

- Try doing your thinking, reflecting and doodling with a drink and maybe a snack. Your brain works better when it's had a glucose refill so you might find you come up with some extra brilliance by accompanying your thinking with a biscuit.[3]
- Put your phone away. A recent study showed that even having it on the desk in front of you takes 15 points off the male IQ and 5 points off the female IQ. If you are going to take 5 or 10 minutes a day to try to improve your thinking, why do something that makes you less clever whilst you do so?[4]

You will notice that some of the activities appear in the journal more than once. Don't worry it's not a misprint! There are 2 reasons:

- The science suggests that if you do something more than once, you are likely to remember it better.
- For some of the activities even greater benefits were found when the activity was repeated over time.

For example, with Gratitude Lists (pages 2 and 38), the study found that people experienced a good result within 4 weeks of writing down grateful thoughts, but that even greater benefits come after 12 weeks. We can't manage to fit in 12 weeks' worth of pages for a single activity here, but hopefully repeating some of the activities exactly or repeating some with different questions to prompt you, should help the idea of them to stick and bring you more benefits than doing them just once.

Where an activity is repeated we have used to show this.

3. ISRAELI PAROLE BOARD. INBRS **P.52**
4. TWINSTITUTE. INBRS **P.51**

HOW THIS BOOK WORKS

Even though the activities are different, I have explained each one in the same structured way. This means that even if the activity is new, it won't take you more than a minute of your precious reflection and thinking time to understand what to actually do. You will see these 3 section headers on every page:

WHAT'S THE POINT?

At the start of each activity is a brief explanation of the science or research that has inspired it. I've kept it super-brief.
There is a reference to the relevant chapter and pages in It's Not Bloody Rocket Science in the bottom left corner of each page. This means that if you want more information, you know where to find it.

LET'S DO IT!

These are the instructions for the activity itself.

REFLECT & QUESTION

These are things to ask yourself once you have done the activity in order to deepen your understanding about your words or doodles.

You will see that each page also includes:

"TOP RIGHT" QUESTION

A question to provoke your thinking in the Top Right corner of each double page. If you want to know more about why I call them Top Right Questions, check out Chapter 9 in It's Not Bloody Rocket Science.

UNDERLYING QUOTE

I've always collected words and phrases. Sadly, at a pub quiz I can be relied upon to know some pretty obscure lyrics from most of the singles released in the 80s and 90s! I have restricted myself here to a quote at the bottom of the page that I think sums up what the exercise is all about.

PARTING SHOT

This is the one thing I would suggest you do as a result of taking the time out to do the activity. Something that should take what you have learnt off the page and help you to make a small but significant change in your life elsewhere – either at home or at work.

It's pretty unusual for writers to allow you to willingly copy their pages! However, I want to positively encourage you to do so – and to use and share the exercises with other people.

If you would like some help to do these activities with your team please have a look at the resources page at www.teabreaktraining.com or get in touch at hello@teabreaktraining.com

If it makes perfect sense to you without our help, then please crack on and spread the word!

CONTENTS

SPECIFIC ACTIVITIES FOR PARTICULAR SITUATIONS

IF YOU ARE FEELING A BIT LOW OR EMOTIONAL TRY THESE ACTIVITIES:

GRATITUDE 123

GRATITUDE LETTER

IMPROVE YOUR JUDGEMENT

HECKLERS – RELEASE SOME BRAIN SPACE

YOU HAVE A BIG DECISION TO MAKE,

IMPROVE YOUR JUDGEMENT

SUCCESS BEYOND MY WILDEST DREAMS

THINK THE OPPOSITE

REFLECTION FRAME: MY BEST LIFE

YOU HAVE AN IDEA... BUT AREN'T SURE WHAT TO DO NEXT

JUST TAKE 10

SUCCESS BEYOND MY WILDEST DREAMS

FEEDBACK CHALLENGE

REFLECTION FRAME: MY BEST LIFE

YOU FEEL OVERWHELMED OR IT FEELS LIKE THERE ARE NOT ENOUGH HOURS IN THE DAY

THE 4 Ds

SPHERE OF INFLUENCE

JUST TAKE 10

HECKLERS

YOU'D LIKE MORE INFLUENCE OR FEEL YOU AREN'T BEING LISTENED TO

LISTEN DIFFERENTLY

FEEDBACK CHALLENGE

REFLECTION FRAME: HOW OTHERS MIGHT SEE ME

SPHERE OF INFLUENCE

YOU FEEL FRUSTRATED OR UNAPPRECIATED

FREE WRITE: FRUSTRATIONS

FEEDBACK CHALLENGE

SPHERE OF INFLUENCE

REFLECTION FRAME: SELF TALK

YOU FEEL REALLY MAD OR UPSET WITH SOMEONE OR SOMETHING

PAY ATTENTION TO YOUR BODY

REFLECTION FRAME: HOW OTHERS MIGHT SEE ME

THINK THE OPPOSITE

FEEDBACK CHALLENGE

YOU FEEL STUCK IN A RUT

BIAS BINGO

REFLECTION FRAME: SELF TALK TRACKER

FREE WRITE: MY BEST LIFE

SPHERE OF INFLUENCE

YOU THINK YOU DESERVE A PAY RISE/PROMOTION AND KEEP GETTING KNOCKED BACK

REFLECTION FRAME: HOW OTHERS MIGHT SEE ME

FEEDBACK CHALLENGE

SPHERE OF INFLUENCE

THINK THE OPPOSITE

YOU HAVE A DIFFICULT RELATIONSHIP TO NAVIGATE

LISTEN DIFFERENTLY

FEEDBACK CHALLENGE

REFLECTION FRAME: HOW OTHERS MIGHT SEE ME

PAY ATTENTION TO YOUR BODY

YOU ARE ABOUT TO BEGIN A NEW JOB OR PROJECT

FIRST 100 DAYS

SUCCESS BEYOND YOUR WILDEST DREAMS

LISTEN DIFFERENTLY

GRATITUDE 123

WHAT'S THE POINT?

The University of Berkeley found that thinking about things we are grateful for releases serotonin into the bloodstream. They found that writing those things down gives you a shot of dopamine as well. Increasing our level of these chemicals improves our mood and could protect against some mental health issues.

LET'S DO IT!

The research found that to feel the full effects, you need 12 weeks, but even after a few days you can feel better. Use the spaces provided to write down 3 things a day. You can either do this over 5 consecutive days or do it once or twice per week. Perhaps there is a particularly good point in your week to put time in your diary for this activity?

THE THINGS THAT ARE REALLY COOL IN MY LIFE THAT I AM GRATEFUL FOR ARE: (IN NO PARTICULAR ORDER)

1. . . . .
. . . .

2. . . . .
. . . .

3. . . . .
. . . .

1. . . . .
. . . .

2. . . . .
. . . .

3. . . . .
. . . .

SELIGMAN ET AL.
2005

"REFLECT UPON YOUR PRESENT BLESSINGS, OF WHICH EVERY MAN HAS PLENTY; NOT ON YOUR PAST MISFORTUNES, OF WHICH ALL MEN HAVE SOME." **CHARLES DICKENS**

WHAT DID I
MISS YESTERDAY
THAT IF I HAD PAID
ATTENTION TO WOULD
HAVE MADE ME
FEEL GOOD?

1. . . . .

2. . . . .

3. . . . .

1. . . . .

2. . . . .

3. . . . .

1. . . . .

2. . . . .

3. . . . .

REFLECT & QUESTION

In what ways did you notice that you felt
better after the activity? Were there any
patterns about the types of things you
were grateful for? If so, how could
you invest more time to experience
these good things more often?

PARTING SHOT

This takes less than a minute
to do each day. Could you
share this science with
someone who it might help?

SPHERE OF INFLUENCE

WHAT'S THE POINT?

Our brain energy is precious and limited. We can easily waste it by spending time on unproductive thoughts that don't make us feel good and don't change anything.

LET'S DO IT!

Think about everything you spent a significant amount of time thinking about today or yesterday. Using the space in the circles below, put each of those chunks of thinking into the relevant circle.

REFLECT & QUESTION

What has this activity helped you to realise?

"WORRY IS JUST IMAGINATION USED IN AN UNPRODUCTIVE WAY."
ANDY ANDREWS

IS THINKING
ABOUT A
RE-OCCURRING ISSUE
SOMETHING YOU SHOULD
CONTINUE TO "RENT"
SPACE TO IN YOUR
HEAD?

HOW COULD I LEARN
TO LIVE WITH THIS?

IS THIS THE BEST
USE OF MY TIME?

WHAT COULD
I DO TODAY?

CAN CONTROL

CAN INFLUENCE

CAN'T CONTROL OR INFLUENCE

PARTING SHOT

What single thing could
you do to make your
thinking more productive
today and tomorrow?

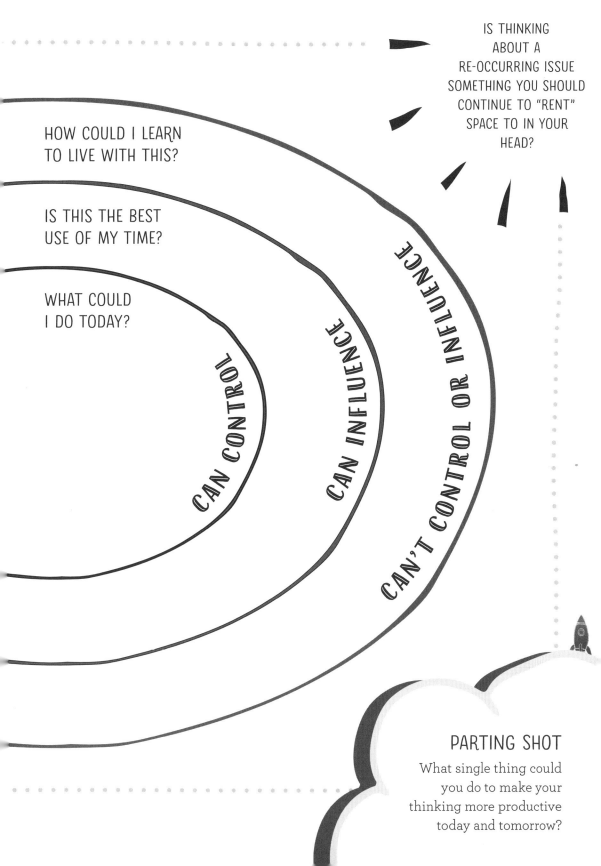

THE 4 Ds

WHAT'S THE POINT?

Writing a To Do list takes time – and it's not always time well invested. Many people report that they simply move tasks they don't want to do from one list to another. Think about the time you could save if you simply did 2 of the things you are putting off right now – rather than take the time to add them to a list...

1. DO IT NOW

2. DIARISE

"START BY DOING WHAT IS NECESSARY; THEN DO WHAT IS POSSIBLE; AND SUDDENLY YOU ARE DOING THE IMPOSSIBLE." **FRANCIS OF ASSISI**

LET'S DO IT!

Take your To Do list. Put every task into one of the following boxes instead. Have a go at this for today...

3. DELEGATE

4. DITCH

REFLECT & QUESTION

Which activities have you been avoiding? Who could give you good feedback on how to improve the effectiveness of your delegation? What would make you too afraid to "ditch" something?

PARTING SHOT

What single thing could you start to do today or tomorrow to make your time more productive?

FEEDBACK CHALLENGE

WHAT'S THE POINT?

Our brain goes for comfort over challenge every time. It tries to conserve energy by making us more attracted to the familiar things and people that we are comfortable with. This is an exercise designed to make you deliberately uncomfortable so that you can observe how that feels - and see if your brain plays any tricks on you to talk you out of doing it!

LET'S DO IT!

Choose someone that you would not normally ask for feedback – maybe you are intimidated by them or don't really get on. Call, email or physically go and see them.

Ask them for feedback about a recent interaction or piece of work you have done together. Thank them for it – even if it is harsh!

Write their feedback opposite and immediately afterwards write down your reaction to it.

A QUESTION THAT MIGHT GET YOU STARTED COULD BE...

"I WOULD REALLY VALUE YOUR FEEDBACK ABOUT YESTERDAY. COULD YOU TELL ME WHAT I DID THAT WAS HELPFUL TO YOU AND WHAT WAS LESS HELPFUL OR YOU WOULD HAVE LIKED ME TO DO DIFFERENTLY?"

INBRS
CHAPTER 1
P.40–42

"WE ALL NEED PEOPLE WHO WILL GIVE US FEEDBACK.
THAT'S HOW WE IMPROVE." **BILL GATES**

WHAT MIGHT
I NOT KNOW, OR
NOT WANT TO KNOW,
WHICH IF I COULD
KNOW, MIGHT
HELP ME?

THEIR RESPONSE

. . . .

. . . .

. . . .

. . . .

YOUR PRIVATE REFLECTIONS ON
HOW IT FELT AND WHAT YOU LEARNT

. . . .

. . . .

. . . .

. . . .

REFLECT & QUESTION

How did it make you feel?
What do you learn about them
and you?

PARTING SHOT

What could you do for the next
week to make sure you are getting
the very best feedback possible –
particularly from people who don't
see the world the way that you do?

FREE WRITING: FRUSTRATIONS

WHAT'S THE POINT?

Normally when we communicate, we make our thoughts sound rational or socially acceptable. Free writing helps us see what is in our subconscious – without it being sanitised. It can be useful for releasing pent up emotions or to help you identify unproductive thoughts.

LET'S DO IT!

There is a big blank space opposite. Take a subject that is currently frustrating you. Use quite small writing and begin to write what you think and feel about the situation. The main thing is not to stop! Don't worry about punctuation, making sense or sanitising what you say because it sounds weird, ugly or strange. Just write.

"TODAY IS THE TOMORROW WE WORRIED ABOUT YESTERDAY." **ANON**

IF YOU COULD
GIVE VOICE TO YOUR
DEEPEST FEARS AND
MOST AMBITIOUS DREAMS
WHAT WOULD YOU HEAR
YOURSELF SAYING?

REFLECT & QUESTION

Now you have filled the pages with words,
read them back. You can choose to read them
back right now, or sleep on it.
Is anything surprising?

What do you notice about what you focus on?

Is this situation something you can control,
influence or need to learn to live with?

PARTING SHOT

What is one thing you
could do right away to
make this situation just
a little bit less
frustrating?

TOP RIGHT QUESTIONS

WHAT'S THE POINT?

Coaching is a technique to help people to think more effectively and fulfil their potential. A good coach will ask tough and challenging questions, but in a safe environment and phrased in a sensitive way so that the brain of the person being asked the questions doesn't get defensive. The trick is to ask questions that someone is curious enough to answer. It can be harder to ask yourself the same questions, without the help of a coach. However, it is often helpful as a way to expand your thinking and create additional options you could consider.

LET'S DO IT

This is an activity over 4 pages that might take you a bit more time to think about. You may want to save it for when you are in a particularly reflective mood or have something especially important on your mind.

There is a question in the Top Right corner of each page of this book. Have a quick flick through. There are several more at the top of this page and more again at TopRightQuestions.com.

Choose a question. Write your initial answer in the space opposite. Don't worry if it seems random, short or incomplete.

"YOU EITHER WALK INSIDE YOUR STORY AND OWN IT OR YOU STAND OUTSIDE YOUR STORY AND HUSTLE FOR YOUR WORTHINESS." BRENE BROWN

TOP RIGHT QUESTIONS CONTINUED

Now we are going to try to get your subconscious working hard by repeating just 2 additional simple questions – either "Tell me more?" or "What Else?" This will enable you to dig deeper into your subconscious.

TELL ME MORE?

With time and space to think and no judgement, you should be able to find out more than you initially thought you knew about the situation you are facing.

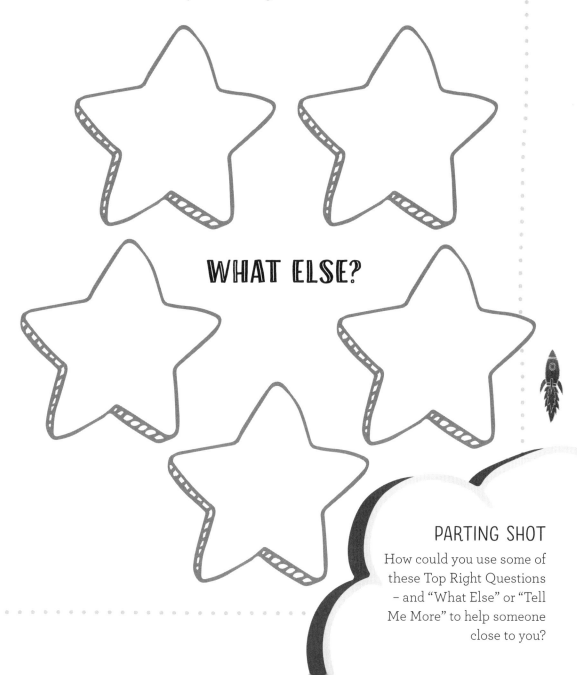

WHAT ELSE?

PARTING SHOT

How could you use some of these Top Right Questions – and "What Else" or "Tell Me More" to help someone close to you?

THINK THE OPPOSITE

WHAT'S THE POINT?

Our brains are subject to cognitive bias. This means we find it difficult to process information which contradicts something we already believe to be true. When you find yourself with a problem to solve or a decision to make, it can help if we force our brains to see what could happen if we held the opposite belief.

LET'S DO IT!

Take a situation that you are certain about your position on, even though you know there are different and strong views to the contrary. This could be about work, your personal life or the wider world. Maybe you want to do something that other people don't seem willing to support? Or you have disagreed with someone because you feel they are just wrong, wrong, wrong. Or it could be something you have decided not to do, because you are certain it is too risky. This exercise can work for any of those things. On the opposite page, summarise in 3 short sentences why you feel that you are right.

Now, on the next page Brainstorm all the possible ways in which you might be wrong. Don't stop until you have filled in the space. Be provocative and challenging. Really try and be clever about taking up the opposing view. Try to stand in someone else's shoes who sees the world differently. Your brain will resist so don't be surprised if it is hard. That's why we've given this activity 4 pages!

"FACED WITH THE CHOICE BETWEEN CHANGING ONE'S MIND AND PROVING THAT THERE IS NO NEED TO DO SO, ALMOST EVERYONE GETS BUSY ON THE PROOF." JK GALBRAITH (HARVARD ECONOMIST)

HOW WOULD YOU WIN AN ARGUMENT WITH YOURSELF THAT THE OPPOSITE WAS TRUE?

3 SENTENCES THAT SUMMARISE WHY I AM COMPLETELY RIGHT

1. . . . .

. . . .

. . . .

. . . .

2. . . . .

. . . .

. . . .

. . . .

3. . . . .

. . . .

. . . .

. . . .

THINK THE OPPOSITE CONTINUED

2 FULL PAGES OF BRAINSTORMING
ABOUT WHY I AM COMPLETELY WRONG...
WHY THE OPPOSITE IS ACTUALLY TRUE
AND I JUST HAVEN'T SEEN IT YET...

"A GOOD COMPROMISE IS ONE WHERE EVERYBODY
MAKES A CONTRIBUTION." ANGELA MERKEL

REFLECT & QUESTION

What is interesting about how you approached why you might be wrong?

What might you have missed thinking about if you had not done this exercise?

What are your Options?

PARTING SHOT

What action could you take right now to make the time on this exercise worthwhile? Examples might include apologising to someone, acknowledging you need more time or information to make a balanced decision, or actually doing something because you are now even more convinced you should!

SUCCESS BEYOND MY WILDEST DREAMS

WHAT'S THE POINT?

Our brains are cognitive misers. They are wired to conserve energy. This can be a good thing (imagine if you noticed every blade of grass or remembered every conversation you'd ever had?) The downside is that we are biased towards the status quo because thinking about something new takes up more energy so our brain resists spending time on it – unless forced.

LET'S DO IT!

Think of something that could be improved in your life, but isn't "broken" as such. Maybe you have the beginnings of a new idea? Or a niggling frustration? Write down all the potential opportunities that could arise if this new idea didn't just work but was amazing; if this frustration didn't just go away but suddenly changed so that you were free to do all sorts of additional things.

"THE TWO MOST IMPORTANT DAYS IN YOUR LIFE ARE THE DAY YOU ARE BORN AND THE DAY YOU FIND OUT WHY." **MARK TWAIN**

THINK SOME MORE. WHAT IS THE VERY BEST THING THAT COULD HAPPEN?

AND SOME MORE. WHAT ELSE COULD HAPPEN? AND WHAT LEFT-FIELD OR ENTIRELY DIFFERENT THINGS COULD THIS LEAD TO?

REFLECT & QUESTION

What could happen in your wildest dreams as a result of taking action? What might stop you?

How could you reduce the risks?

PARTING SHOT

What is one small step you could take right now to do something that would get you closer to your dream not being so wild after all?

JUST TAKE 10

WHAT'S THE POINT?

When we are tired or putting things off, our brains can go into overdrive and come up with some really fantastic excuses to stop us making progress. "I don't have time." "It won't work." "People won't like it". These excuses will sound compelling because your brain has invented them just for you. Problem is, they might not be true...

LET'S DO IT!

Pick a task you have been putting off or an idea you can't find the time to expand upon. Set a timer for 10 minutes. You are going to work on it for just that 10 minutes in a series of 2 minute "sprints". Set the timer before your clever brain can find you 10 convincing reasons that you don't have time...

0 TO 2 MINUTE SPRINT:

Write down the benefits of doing this job or implementing this new idea. Think of more benefits to fill the time – even if they sound quite silly.

Break the task or idea down into 3 distinct chunks. Maybe PLAN, DO, REVIEW or STEP 1, STEP 2, STEP 3.

2 TO 4 MINUTE SPRINT:

"YOU'VE GOT TO GET UP EVERY MORNING WITH DETERMINATION IF YOU'RE GOING TO GO TO BED WITH SATISFACTION." **GEORGE LORIMER**

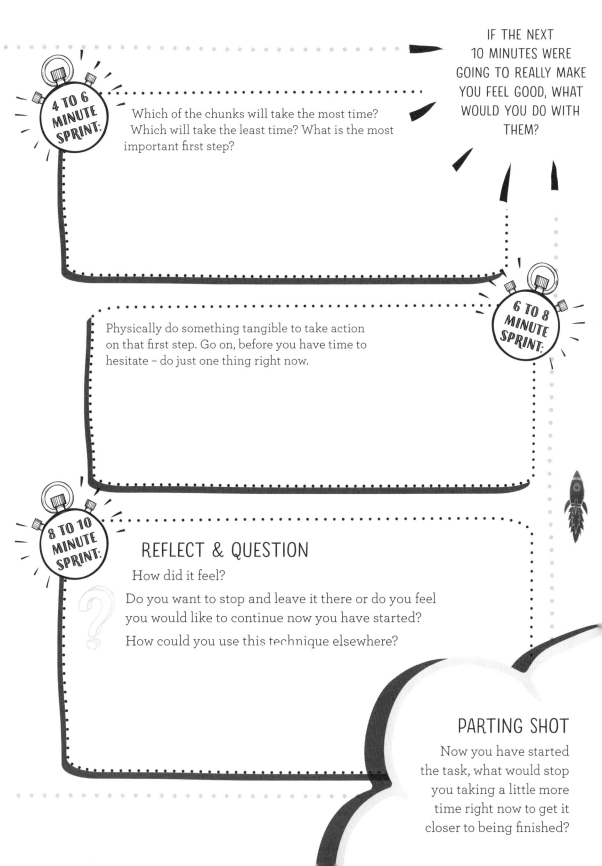

4 TO 6 MINUTE SPRINT:

Which of the chunks will take the most time? Which will take the least time? What is the most important first step?

IF THE NEXT 10 MINUTES WERE GOING TO REALLY MAKE YOU FEEL GOOD, WHAT WOULD YOU DO WITH THEM?

6 TO 8 MINUTE SPRINT:

Physically do something tangible to take action on that first step. Go on, before you have time to hesitate – do just one thing right now.

8 TO 10 MINUTE SPRINT:

REFLECT & QUESTION

How did it feel?

Do you want to stop and leave it there or do you feel you would like to continue now you have started?

How could you use this technique elsewhere?

PARTING SHOT

Now you have started the task, what would stop you taking a little more time right now to get it closer to being finished?

REFLECTION FRAME: SELF TALK

WHAT'S THE POINT?

We have an almost non-stop dialogue with ourselves. It can pay dividends to take a deliberate pause and think about what your "inner voice" is saying. What tone of voice do you speak to yourself in? What phrases do you use when speaking to yourself? This can help us to understand if our inner voice is being constructive and balanced or over-critical and unhelpful.

WHAT HAVE YOU NOTICED ABOUT YOUR THOUGHTS ABOUT YOURSELF OR YOUR "SELF-TALK"?

WHAT POSITIVE THINGS HAVE YOU TOLD YOURSELF OR OTHER PEOPLE ABOUT YOUR WORK/EFFORTS OR YOURSELF SO FAR TODAY?

HAVE YOU IMAGINED THE FUTURE AND WHAT MIGHT HAPPEN AS A RESULT OF YOUR ACTIONS? – DID YOU IMAGINE POSITIVE OR NEGATIVE THINGS HAPPENING?

LET'S DO IT!

Take a photo or photocopy of this page as it's ideal if you can do this activity throughout the day. Set a timer on your watch or phone so that it goes off once per hour. When the alarm goes off, use the questions around the outside of the reflection frame in order to make some comments in the centre of the page. You don't need hours, 2 minutes might do. Be honest and non-judgemental. Try to write instinctively without editing or over-thinking.

REFLECT & QUESTION

What patterns do you see? Do you notice anything about time of day or different interactions or people influencing your self-talk?

What would you say to a friend if this was their self-talk?

HAVE YOU NOTICED ANYTHING YOU DID OR DIDN'T DO SO FAR TODAY BECAUSE YOU WERE WORRIED ABOUT FAILING OR WHAT OTHER PEOPLE MIGHT THINK?

WHAT NEGATIVE THINGS HAVE YOU TOLD YOURSELF OR OTHER PEOPLE ABOUT YOUR WORK/EFFORTS OR SELF SO FAR TODAY?

PARTING SHOT

What single small step could you practise tomorrow that would be positive for you?

. . . .

. . . .

. . . .

GRATITUDE LETTER

WHAT'S THE POINT?

There is good science out there that shows that writing down the things we are grateful for can release the feel-good chemicals serotonin and dopamine into the blood stream. Random acts of kindness can add to the release and make others feel good too. What's not to like?

LET'S DO IT!

Use this page to write a letter to someone to say thanks for something. It could be someone you met yesterday. Or a teacher from school you haven't seen for 20 years...

We have left the reverse of the page opposite blank. That way you can rip out the whole page and send it to the person you are grateful to, without losing any other content. Or use it to write a longer letter if you have a lot to say "thanks" for!

EDMONDS AND
MCCULLOGH
2003

"I REGARD GRATITUDE AS AN ASSET AND IT'S
ABSENCE AS A MAJOR INTERPERSONAL FLAW."
MARSHALL GOLDSMITH

Dear...

IF I WAS GOING
TO BE AT MY MOST
HAPPY AND MY MOST
PRODUCTIVE, WHO SHOULD
I SPEND MORE AND WHO
SHOULD I SPEND LESS
TIME WITH?

REFLECT & QUESTION

What emotions did writing this letter evoke?

Pause and notice... How do you feel now?

How would you feel if you received a similar letter in the post tomorrow?

What small actions could you take today that might grow into you receiving such a letter in the future?

PARTING SHOT

For additional brain boosting chemicals, take a picture when you are done, track them down on social media and send it as a photo? Or rip out the page and send it snail mail.

HECKLERS – RELEASE SOME BRAIN SPACE

WHAT'S THE POINT?

The things that we keep putting off or need to remember to do, have a rather irritating habit of popping into our heads when we are trying to relax or concentrate on something important.

I call these "hecklers". Imagine you are a performer on the stage of your own life, these distracting thoughts keep shouting "don't forget me..." just as you are starting to relax or want to get excited about a new project. Because our brains are less productive when we are trying to do more than one thing at once, having "hecklers" is a waste of our precious brain energy.

LET'S DO IT

Write down 5 tasks or things that you need to remember to do which, rather irritatingly, keep popping up into your head when you are trying to relax or concentrate on something important.

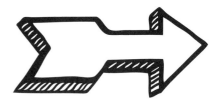

REFLECT & QUESTION

Think about your list. Are there any items on the list that if you did them right now, would be done, dusted and off your list? OK. Here is the challenge. Do 1 or 2 of them right now! Or maybe feel fantastic and do all 5?!

"THOSE WHO SAY IT CANNOT BE DONE SHOULD NOT INTERRUPT THOSE DOING IT!" **GEORGE BERNARD SHAW**

1 ....

....

....

2 ....

....

....

3 ....

....

....

4 ....

....

....

5 ....

....

....

PARTING SHOT

Remember that if a
"heckler" pops into your
head more than once, it is
something you have wasted
precious brain energy on.

LISTEN DIFFERENTLY

WHAT'S THE POINT?

There are generally accepted to be 4 different ways in which we can listen when other people are talking. However, we can often fall into the trap of just listening to respond – rather than to understand. When we actively focus on how we are listening, we can pick up different information. This can help decision making and to build more trusting relationships.

LET'S DO IT

Find an occasion when your listening can be quite passive – perhaps during a long meeting or discussion when the content does not directly impact you.

You are going to actively try to listen in 4 very different ways. Try to switch between these different modes of listening in turn. Try to isolate them and do them one at a time. Notice what information you gain by listening differently each time.

REFLECT & QUESTION

What different things did you notice when you used the 4 different modes of listening? Which modes did you find easy? Which might you need to practise to do more of?

1 LISTEN FOR FACTS AND INFORMATION

Tune into what facts and information someone is sharing with you. Note down what you are being told – taking it at face value only

2 LISTEN TO ANALYSE

Think about what the person is saying. Consider if you agree or disagree. What are the implications of what you are being told? If you were going to be helpfully critical of their views how would you express that?

"MOST PEOPLE DO NOT LISTEN WITH THE INTENT TO UNDERSTAND; THEY LISTEN WITH THE INTENT TO REPLY." **STEPHEN R. COVEY**

3 LISTEN FOR EMOTION/FEELINGS

Tune out completely from the facts and information or what you personally think or feel about the implications. What body language, volume and tone are they using? What might that suggest they are feeling about the situation they are describing?

4 LISTEN INTUITIVELY

Now don't listen for facts, to criticise or for feelings. Simply tune into to your intuition as someone is speaking. What are they not saying? What is the underlying message they are giving you or others?

PARTING SHOT

Do you have an important listening occasion coming up such as hosting an interview or a difficult conversation? How could you remember to use these different modes of listening to enhance that conversation?

SPHERE OF INFLUENCE

WHAT'S THE POINT?

Our brain energy is precious and limited. We can easily waste it by spending time on unproductive thoughts that don't make us feel good and don't change anything.

LET'S DO IT!

Think about everything you spent a significant amount of time thinking about today or yesterday. Using the space in the circles below, put each of those chunks of thinking into the relevant circle.

REFLECT & QUESTION

What has this activity helped you to realise?

INBRS
CHAPTER 7
P.155–159

"FORGET YESTERDAY – IT HAS ALREADY FORGOTTEN YOU. DON'T SWEAT TOMORROW – YOU HAVEN'T EVEN MET. INSTEAD, OPEN YOUR EYES AND YOUR HEART TO A TRULY PRECIOUS GIFT – TODAY." **STEVE MARABOLI**

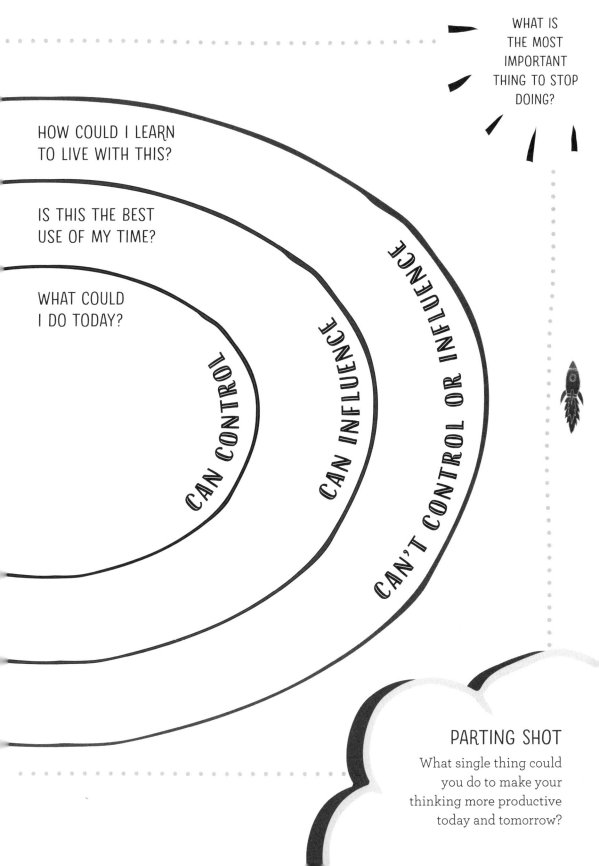

WHAT IS THE MOST IMPORTANT THING TO STOP DOING?

HOW COULD I LEARN TO LIVE WITH THIS?

IS THIS THE BEST USE OF MY TIME?

WHAT COULD I DO TODAY?

CAN CONTROL

CAN INFLUENCE

CAN'T CONTROL OR INFLUENCE

PARTING SHOT

What single thing could you do to make your thinking more productive today and tomorrow?

IMPROVE YOUR JUDGEMENT

WHAT'S THE POINT?

You might be surprised to know that if you do an activity to affirm your self-worth before you analyse some information to make a decision, you will do a better job. Research shows you will be much more able to read data such as tables, graphs, numbers etc. and see it at face value without your natural biases affecting you, if you have spent a few moments affirming your self-worth first...

LET'S DO IT!

Use the space to write about an experience that made you feel good about yourself.

What did you do?

How did others respond?

What was it about what you did that made you feel good?

Have you repeated this – or something similar? If so, did it make you feel good a second time?

"YOUR SOUL NEEDS TIME FOR SOLITUDE AND SELF-REFLECTION. IN ORDER TO LOVE, LEAD, HEAL, AND CREATE, YOU MUST NOURISH YOURSELF FIRST." **LOUISE HAY**

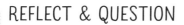

REFLECT & QUESTION

How did doing that activity make you feel?

Are there any downsides to thinking back to things you did which made you feel good about yourself?

PARTING SHOT

How could you remember to do this activity for 2 or 3 minutes prior to the next time that you have to evaluate some information or data and need to have an open mind?

GRATITUDE 123

WHAT'S THE POINT?

The University of Berkeley found that thinking about things we are grateful for releases serotonin into the bloodstream. They found that writing those things down gives you a shot of dopamine as well. Increasing our level of these chemicals improves our mood and could protect against some mental health issues.

LET'S DO IT!

The research found that to feel the full effects, you need 12 weeks, but even after a few days you can feel better. Use the spaces provided to write down 3 things a day. You can either do this over 5 consecutive days or do it once or twice per week. Perhaps there is a particularly good point in your week to put time in your diary for this activity?

THE THINGS THAT ARE REALLY COOL IN MY LIFE THAT I AM GRATEFUL FOR ARE: (IN NO PARTICULAR ORDER)

1. . . . .
. . . .

2. . . . .
. . . .

3. . . . .
. . . .

1. . . . .
. . . .

2. . . . .
. . . .

3. . . . .
. . . .

SELIGMAN ET AL.
2005

"THIS IS A WONDERFUL DAY. I'VE NEVER SEEN THIS ONE BEFORE."
MAYA ANGELOU

1. . . . .

2. . . . .

3. . . . .

1. . . . .

2. . . . .

3. . . . .

1. . . . .

2. . . . .

3. . . . .

REFLECT & QUESTION

In what ways did you notice that you felt
better after the activity? Were there any
patterns about the types of things you
were grateful for? If so, how could
you invest more time to experience
these good things more often?

PARTING SHOT

This takes less than a minute
to do each day. Could you
share this science with
someone who it might help?

JUST TAKE 10

WHAT'S THE POINT?

When we are tired or putting things off, our brains can go into overdrive and come up with some really fantastic excuses to stop us making progress. "I don't have time." "It won't work." "People won't like it". These excuses will sound compelling because your brain has invented them just for you. Problem is, they might not be true...

LET'S DO IT!

Pick a task you have been putting off or an idea you can't find the time to expand upon. Set a timer for 10 minutes. You are going to work on it for just that 10 minutes in a series of 2 minute "sprints". Set the timer before your clever brain can find you 10 convincing reasons that you don't have time...

0 TO 2 MINUTE SPRINT:

Write down the benefits of doing this job or implementing this new idea. Think of more benefits to fill the time – even if they sound quite silly.

Break the task or idea down into 3 distinct chunks.
Maybe PLAN, DO, REVIEW or STEP 1, STEP 2, STEP 3.

2 TO 4 MINUTE SPRINT:

"I DIDN'T GET THERE BY WISHING FOR IT OR HOPING FOR IT, BUT BY WORKING FOR IT." ESTÉE LAUDER

4 TO 6 MINUTE SPRINT:

Which of the chunks will take the most time?
Which will take the least time? What is the most
important first step?

6 TO 8 MINUTE SPRINT:

Physically do something tangible to take action
on that first step. Go on, before you have time to
hesitate – do just one thing right now.

8 TO 10 MINUTE SPRINT:

REFLECT & QUESTION

How did it feel?

Do you want to stop and leave it there or do you feel
you would like to continue now you have started?

How could you use this technique elsewhere?

PARTING SHOT

Now you have started
the task, what would stop
you taking a little more
time right now to get it
closer to being finished?

THREAT ALERT: PAY ATTENTION TO YOUR BODY

WHAT'S THE POINT?

When someone intimidates us, makes us feel threatened or challenges what we feel is fair or reasonable, a physiological reaction occurs in our body.

Maybe you go red in the face or get a flush creeping up your neck? Maybe you get pins and needles in your feet? Maybe you get a churning stomach? Maybe you feel a particular part of your body tense up?

Most of the reactions you can see or feel require blood and oxygen to rush to this localised area of your body. The flush on your neck and cheeks is the result of your capillaries in your face widening to allow more blood to flow to that area - to the extent that you can see it through your skin! The muscle tension you feel in your legs or shoulders requires more blood and oxygen to go to that area. Most of us don't walk round with an oxygen tank and a blood transfusion machine and we can't create fresh blood and oxygen as quickly as we need it. This means that part of your body is be temporarily depleted of blood and oxygen in order to fulfil the additional need in your cheeks, leg or shoulders. Neuroscientific research has identified that the part of your body that is temporarily starved is your brain...specifically the bit of your brain that deals with problem solving, memory recall and decision making. This is why your mind goes blank sometimes when someone asks you a question or does something that makes you feel threatened. You literally can't think – because the blood and oxygen that would allow you to think is in your hands, feet or cheeks instead!

LET'S DO IT

Draw a picture of yourself showing the physical reaction that you experience in the frame opposite. Make the part of your body that experiences the rush of blood really big. Make your brain really small in the picture.

It really doesn't have to be a masterpiece – a stick man will do!

INBRS
CHAPTER 5
P.112

"NO ONE CAN MAKE YOU FEEL INFERIOR WITHOUT YOUR CONSENT."
ELEANOR ROOSEVELT

IF I WANTED TO CHALLENGE MORE AND THREATEN LESS, WHAT WOULD I DO?

REFLECT & QUESTION

When this reaction happens, the best thing to do is take a breath. To buy some time so that your body can suck the blood and oxygen back to where it belongs.

How could you remind yourself it's normal to struggle to think clearly when you have a cheek flush or tense shoulders?

PARTING SHOT

Write down 2 things that you could try to do the next time this happens to you. Keep your ideas REALLY simple so that your blood and oxygen depleted brain can remember them!

DO IT AGAIN

GRATITUDE LETTER

WHAT'S THE POINT?

There is good science out there that shows that writing down the things we are grateful for can release the feel-good chemicals serotonin and dopamine into the blood stream. Random acts of kindness can add to the release and make others feel good too. What's not to like?

LET'S DO IT!

Use this page to write a letter to someone to say thanks for something. It could be someone you met yesterday. Or a teacher from school you haven't seen for 20 years...

We have left the reverse of the page opposite blank. That way you can rip out the whole page and send it to the person you are grateful to, without losing any other content. Or use it to write a longer letter if you have a lot to say "thanks" for!

EDMONDS AND
MCCULLOGH
2003

"ONE CAN NEVER PAY IN GRATITUDE; ONE CAN ONLY PAY 'IN KIND' SOMEWHERE ELSE IN LIFE." **ANNE MORROW LINDBERGH**

Dear...

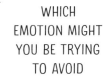

REFLECT & QUESTION

What emotions did writing this letter evoke?

Pause and notice... How do you feel now?

How would you feel if you received a similar letter in the post tomorrow?

What small actions could you take today that might grow into you receiving such a letter in the future?

PARTING SHOT

For additional brain boosting chemicals, take a picture when you are done, track them down on social media and send it as a photo? Or rip out the page and send it snail mail.

REFLECTION FRAME: HOW OTHERS SEE ME

WHAT'S THE POINT?

Research suggests we make a first impression in 7 seconds and give off more than 800 non-verbal cues or clues about what we are thinking and feeling every 30 minutes. It can pay dividends to take a deliberate pause and think about what other people are hearing when we are speaking. What are others seeing when we walk into a room or they are sat with us?

WHAT HAVE YOU NOTICED ABOUT YOUR CONVERSATIONS OR INTERACTIONS WITH PEOPLE SO FAR TODAY?

WHAT POSITIVE THINGS HAVE YOU TOLD OTHER PEOPLE ABOUT THEIR WORK/ EFFORTS OR THEMSELVES SO FAR TODAY?

DO YOU THINK ANYONE HAS HAD ANY STRONG REACTIONS TO YOU TODAY? LIKED YOU? DISLIKED YOU? BEEN IRRITATED BY YOU? LOVED YOU? BEEN IMPRESSED BY YOU? BEEN DISAPPOINTED IN YOU? BEEN INTIMIDATED BY YOU? BEEN FRUSTRATED BY YOU?

LET'S DO IT!

Take a photo or photocopy of this page as it's ideal if you can do this activity throughout the day. Set a timer on your watch or phone so that it goes off once per hour. When the alarm goes off, use the questions around the outside of the reflection frame in order to make some comments in the centre of the page. You don't need hours. 2 minutes might do. Be honest and non- judgemental. Try to write instinctively without editing or over-thinking.

REFLECT & QUESTION

Do you think people get the same impression of you that you were hoping to give them? Do you notice anything about time of day or different interactions or people influencing how you interact or behave around people?

How could you influence people better or improve your relationships with them?

What could you do a little more of and a little less of today in order for other people to see the version of yourself that you would want them to?

HAVE YOU NOTICED ANYTHING YOU DID OR DIDN'T DO SO FAR TODAY THAT SEEMED TO HAVE HAD NEGATIVE IMPACT ON ANYONE OR THEIR DAY?

HAVE YOU DONE ANYTHING KIND TODAY?

PARTING SHOT

What single small step could you practise tomorrow that would be positive for you?

. . . .

. . . .

. . . .

WHAT FEEDBACK HAVE YOU GIVEN OTHER PEOPLE TODAY. WAS IT POSITIVE FEEDBACK OR NEGATIVE FEEDBACK? HOW DID YOU DO?

TOP RIGHT QUESTIONS

WHAT'S THE POINT?

Coaching is a technique to help people to think more effectively and fulfil their potential. A good coach will ask tough and challenging questions, but in a safe environment and phrased in a sensitive way so that the brain of the person being asked the questions doesn't get defensive. The trick is to ask questions that someone is curious enough to answer. It can be harder to ask yourself the same questions, without the help of a coach. However, it is often helpful as a way to expand your thinking and create additional options you could consider.

LET'S DO IT

This is an activity over 4 pages that might take you a bit more time to think about. You may want to save it for when you are in a particularly reflective mood or have something especially important on your mind.

There is a question in the Top Right corner of each page of this book. Have a quick flick through. There are several more at the top of this page and more again at TopRightQuestions.com.

Choose a question. Write your initial answer in the space opposite. Don't worry if it seems random, short or incomplete.

"WE DO NOT NEED MAGIC TO CHANGE THE WORLD, WE CARRY ALL THE POWER WE NEED INSIDE OURSELVES ALREADY: WE HAVE THE POWER TO IMAGINE BETTER." **J.K. ROWLING**

TOP RIGHT QUESTIONS CONTINUED

Now we are going to try to get your subconscious working hard by repeating just 2 additional simple questions – either "Tell me more?" or "What Else?" This will enable you to dig deeper into your subconscious.

TELL ME MORE?

With time and space to think and no judgement, you should be able to find out more than you initially thought you knew about the situation you are facing.

WHAT ELSE?

PARTING SHOT

How could you use some of these Top Right Questions – and "What Else" or "Tell Me More" to help someone close to you?

DO IT AGAIN

LISTEN DIFFERENTLY

WHAT'S THE POINT?

There are generally accepted to be
4 different ways in which we can listen
when other people are talking.
However, we can often fall into the
trap of just listening to respond –
rather than to understand. When we
actively focus on how we are listening,
we can pick up different information.
This can help decision making and to
build more trusting relationships.

LET'S DO IT

Find an occasion when your listening
can be quite passive – perhaps during
a long meeting or discussion when the
content does not directly impact you.

You are going to actively try to listen
in 4 very different ways. Try to switch
between these different modes of
listening in turn. Try to isolate them
and do them one at a time. Notice
what information you gain by
listening differently each time.

? REFLECT & QUESTION

What different things did you notice
when you used the 4 different modes of
listening? Which modes did you find
easy? Which might you need to practise
to do more of?

1 LISTEN FOR FACTS AND INFORMATION

Tune into what facts and
information someone is sharing
with you. Note down what you
are being told – taking it at face
value only

2 LISTEN TO ANALYSE

Think about what the
person is saying. Consider if
you agree or disagree. What
are the implications of what
you are being told? If you were
going to be helpfully critical of
their views how would you
express that?

*"I NEED TO LISTEN WELL SO THAT I HEAR
WHAT IS NOT SAID." THULI MADONSELA*

3 LISTEN FOR EMOTION/FEELINGS

Tune out completely from the facts and information or what you personally think or feel about the implications. What body language, volume and tone are they using? What might that suggest they are feeling about the situation they are describing?

4 LISTEN INTUITIVELY

Now don't listen for facts, to criticise or for feelings. Simply tune into to your intuition as someone is speaking. What are they not saying? What is the underlying message they are giving you or others?

PARTING SHOT

Do you have an important listening occasion coming up such as hosting an interview or a difficult conversation? How could you remember to use these different modes of listening to enhance that conversation?

THE 4 Ds

WHAT'S THE POINT?

Writing a To Do list takes time – and it's not always time well invested. Many people report that they simply move tasks they don't want to do from one list to another. Think about the time you could save if you simply did 2 of the things you are putting off right now – rather than take the time to add them to a list...

1. DO IT NOW

2. DIARISE

"KNOWING WHAT MUST BE DONE DOES AWAY WITH FEAR." **ROSA PARKS**

LET'S DO IT!

Take your To Do list. Put
every task into one of the
following boxes instead.
Have a go at this for today...

3. DELEGATE

4. DITCH

REFLECT & QUESTION

Which activities have you been
avoiding? Who could give you good
feedback on how to improve the
effectiveness of your delegation?
What would make you too afraid to
"ditch" something?

PARTING SHOT

What single thing could
you start to do today or
tomorrow to make your
time more productive?

BIAS BINGO

WHAT'S THE POINT?

Our brains are wired to make life easier for us by sticking to patterns of thinking that already work for us. This has lots of upsides. But one of the downsides is that we can be restricting our ability to think differently about situations and to therefore limit the potential new scenarios or solutions we could create for ourselves. Spotting where we have some natural biases in our current thought patterns can enable us to challenge ourselves to think better.

LET'S DO IT!

Here is a table with boxes in it. Within each box is a description of something you might say out loud or tell yourself. Spend some time today playing "bingo" – crossing off each box when you notice that your brain is trying to trick you by using a bias to stop you from thinking more broadly.

Maybe treat yourself if you get a line! Maybe treat yourself big if you spot them all and get a full house!

FREQUENCY BIAS
You heard someone say something yesterday or saw someone doing something yesterday and now they (or other people) are saying and doing it all the time

SELF-SERVING BIAS
You find yourself deciding that a quality in someone is not that important because it is something that you have always managed to work around

IN-GROUP BIAS
You find yourself thinking that someone outside your team or family is not as good at something or doesn't possess as much of a quality as someone within your team or family

"MINDS ARE LIKE PARACHUTES, THEY ONLY FUNCTION WHEN THEY ARE OPEN."
SIR THOMAS DEWAR

CURRENT MOMENT BIAS

You find yourself doing something interesting, but not very important/urgent when you have something important/urgent waiting to be done.

NEGATIVITY BIAS

You find yourself thinking that someone being critical of something is smarter than someone who is being positive about something

CONFIRMATION BIAS

You have always thought that this person is a bad/late/disorganised person and they have just proved you right...again

STATUS-QUO BIAS

You find yourself saying "It's not broken, so let's not fix it" without really stopping to think if the fix could be worthwhile

CURRENT MOMENT BIAS

You find yourself putting something off that you don't really want to do and saying "I'll do that tomorrow/another time"

BANDWAGON BIAS

You find yourself using phrases like "everyone thinks that" or "nobody does that"

FREQUENCY BIAS

You find yourself noticing a particular object when you have just bought or looked at buying that object yourself

NEGATIVITY BIAS

You find yourself paying much more attention to a criticism you received than a compliment

CONFIRMATION BIAS

Your best friend or star colleague at work has just done something brilliant. Again.

REFLECT & QUESTION

Did you notice anything different about your thought patterns as a result of doing this activity?

Did the fact that these traits were called "biases" make you more or less likely to spot them?

PARTING SHOT

Try to spot an example of a bias each day for the next week. Challenge it, if you can.

FREE WRITING: MY BEST LIFE

WHAT'S THE POINT?

Normally when we communicate, we make our thoughts sound rational or socially acceptable. Free writing helps us see what is in our subconscious – without it being sanitised. It can be useful for releasing pent up emotions or to help you identify unproductive thoughts.

LET'S DO IT!

Here is a big blank space. Think about what your perfect week would look like and describe it. Use quite small writing and simply begin to write. Think about what you are doing in your perfect week and how it makes you feel. The main thing is not to stop! Don't worry about punctuation, making sense or sanitising what you say because it sounds weird, ugly or strange. Just write.

"BE YOURSELF, EVERYONE ELSE IS ALREADY TAKEN." OSCAR WILDE

IF YOU WERE BEING THE BEST VERSION OF YOURSELF, WHAT WOULD YOU BE DOING RIGHT NOW?

REFLECT & QUESTION

What do you notice when you read this back?

How similar is this to your life right now?

What is really holding you back from planning to have this life?

PARTING SHOT

What is one step you could take right now that would bring your current week more in line with your perfect week?

FIRST 100 DAYS

WHAT'S THE POINT?

When we have a new challenge, we might want to get stuck in straight away! However, it can be really helpful to reflect on what we want to get from it and how we want to feel before we start. You can then plan to get what you want to get, and work out how to make sure you feel how you want to feel. Writing these things out can help to give us clarity and to stop us getting bogged down and exhibiting frustrations or behaviours that might get in the way of the goal.

LET'S DO IT!

Ask yourself the questions on these four pages. If it is a big job or project there might not be enough room here, so feel free to continue on flipcharts or in a separate notebook.

When you are at Day 100 what do you want people to say has happened?. Think about the practical things you want to achieve? What 1 or 2 sentences would enable you to describe this in the time it takes to go up 2 floors in a lift?

THE BOSTON CONSULTING GROUP
BCG.COM

"THERE ARE TWO KINDS OF PEOPLE, THOSE WHO DO THE WORK AND THOSE WHO TAKE THE CREDIT. TRY TO BE IN THE FIRST GROUP; THERE IS LESS COMPETITION THERE." **INDIRA GANDHI**

WHAT VERSION OF MYSELF WOULD DO THIS AND SUCCEED?

What changes do you think you will need to make to the people around you to get the outcome you want and to make sure people feel how you want them to feel?

How will you make sure everyone (upwards, downwards and sideways) understands the plan and sticks to it?

FIRST 100 DAYS CONTINUED

Imagine you are watching your first 100 days back on a video. What language, behaviour, mannerisms and stories will be in your edited highlights which will cement that first impression?

REFLECT & QUESTION

What do you know you will find easy and difficult about achieving your plan?

How could you transfer some of the things you did well in different situations to this new challenge?

When you haven't created a great first impression in the past or didn't get what you wanted, what could you learn from that which might help here?

What is the first impression you want to create as you meet each new team member?

When you are at Day 100 how do you want people to feel about you and about themselves?

How will you make sure that you talk to the right people – inside and outside of your team/company/family – to understand what is really going on

What details will you need to understand more about? Finances? Disputes? Processes? What previous mistakes might you need to rectify quickly?

PARTING SHOT

What could you do first and right now that would increase your chances of success?

A NOTE ON REFERENCES

For those of you who have read It's Not Bloody Rocket Science, you might remember there were 4 pages of references (in very small writing!). I have not repeated them here. In the case of Gratitude and First 100 Days, there are extensive resources on the internet that I don't cover in It's Not Bloody Rocket Science, so I have simply included the names of some of the original thinkers so that you can find their work on the web if you want more information, and work outwards from there.

I want to stress that the activities and ideas in this book are absolutely NOT mine and mine alone. I have been fascinated with the science and research on evolution, leadership and life for over 20 years. Every activity may have been influenced by a number of ideas from many of the brilliant books and articles I have read over that time.

If you are a reader and would like to know more about the original source of an idea, please check out the references in the main book.

I have also included all my references on my website at www.toprightthinking.com so that I can keep them updated regularly. If you are a writer or researcher who feel I have not referenced an idea that you came up with, then please let me know as I would dearly like to put that right.

The Top Right Questions on these pages are not all my own work either. Coaching involves spending a good chunk of your life collecting and curating questions so that we can ask a great question that unlocks someone's thinking. Some of the Top Right Questions in this book were asked of me – and worked so well that they stuck in my mind. Some of the ones you see here were donated to me by people I have helped to train as coaches as part of my blog at toprightquestions.com. I hope that if any of those very talented people see a question that they thought was "theirs" that they will forgive me knowing me as I am – a good coach and trainer, but one without the most efficient filing system in the world...

ACKNOWLEDGEMENTS

Thanks so much to the following people who helped along the way

For supplying their favourite quotes:
Alex Shepherd, Nikki Blackhurst, Kadisha Lewis Roberts, Sarah Collett, Joanne Burton and Alison Bradbury (Ali – Given the need to keep everything neutral there wasn't a perfect place for your favourite quote - but nonetheless, it's now my current favourite too! So thanks so much for "Well behaved women seldom make history." Laurel Thatcher Ulrich. It's now officially my mantra!)

For the Top Right Questions in the book thanks to Kerry Fry, Simon Plumbe, Nikki Yeomans, Amanda Harvey, Caroline Jones, Alex Darby, Nicola Ghodse, Elizabeth Davis, Glenda Wadsworth, Katie White, Andy Smith, Demi van der Venter and all the other coaches who have contributed to the TopRightQuestions project.

Particular thanks to Lyra Cobb, Amelia Swanston and Amelie Cobb who, by providing three of the questions I use most in my professional life, prove what most parents know already – sometimes it is your children who ask you the very best questions of all.

Thanks Darren Entwistle for undertaking proof reading duties – even on holiday!

Claire Maguire – you are a detail conscious legend, which is also why you are the EA from heaven.

Many thanks to Karen Burling who as well as being a fantastic proof reader has helped in so many other ways too. I could list them. But might need another book!

Special thanks to Helen Melvin who as well as being a fabulous advocate for the books has gone out of her way to share her phenomenal eye for detail and her thoughtful way of making challenging suggestions. She literally embodies the values of the organisation she helps to lead.

Thanks to Tom Arundel who despite being in charge of making sure hundreds of people are paid at Christmas, took a full evening out to read and critique and make some great suggestions about tone too. Loving the feedback Tom!

Cheers to Dan at Couper Street Type Co. Literally the best and most helpful person you could hope to meet if you want a book to look gorgeous. And he can surf.

To Sarah. Where do you start? She's literally the best person I know at getting things done in a professional sense and never letting you lose your faith in yourself. The wine bill is close to being always mine to pick up...

And to Jamie, thanks for always skipping to the back of books to find out what happens at the end. A salient lesson in the science that all habits have a use – even the irritating ones x

FINAL PARTING SHOT

If you have got this far by doing all the activities and have got to the end, bravo! Hopefully you feel amazing and have got some ideas about how to fulfil the potential that we both know you have. If the activities have worked you hard, you might already be halfway there!

If you are like my husband and skip to the back of every book when you first pick it up, then please do find the time to go back and read it from the beginning. But maybe with this final quote in mind:

> 'Life should not be a journey to the grave with the intention of arriving safely in a pretty and well preserved body, but rather to skid in broadside in a cloud of smoke, thoroughly used up, totally worn out, and loudly proclaiming "Wow! What a Ride!" '
>
> *Hunter S. Thompson*